SOCCER CHAMPIONS

BY JIM WHITING

REAL MADRID

Published by Creative Education
and Creative Paperbacks
P.O. Box 227, Mankato, Minnesota 56002
Creative Education and Creative Paperbacks
are imprints of The Creative Company
www.thecreativecompany.us

Design and production by The Design Lab
Art direction by Rita Marshall
Printed in Malaysia

Photographs by Corbis ('-'/epa; AP; Sandor Bojar/
epa; Colorsport; KIKO HUESCA/epa; Hulton-Deutsch
Collection; Ian MacNicol/Colorsport; Stephane Mantey/
TempSport; Ivan Abanades Medina/Cordon Press;
Mirrorpix/Splash News; Reuters; Swim Ink 2, LLC;
Universal/TempSport; SUSANA VERA/Reuters), Getty
Images (Rolls Press/Popperfoto, STAFF), photosinbox.
com, Shutterstock (Anton_Ivanov, gualtiero boffi,
KarSol, Denis Kuvaev, Rafael Ramirez Lee, Madridismo.
Org, Maxisport, Morphart Creation, Matt Trommer,
Marcos Mesa Sam Wordley), Wikimedia Creative
Commons (El País, Christian Franzen, KSA13)

Library of Congress Cataloging-in-Publication Data
Whiting, Jim.
Real Madrid / by Jim Whiting.
p. cm. — (Soccer champions)
Includes bibliographical references and index.
Summary: A chronicle of the people, matches,
and world events that shaped the European
men's Spanish soccer team known as Real
Madrid, from its founding in 1902 to today.
ISBN 978-1-60818-591-7 (hardcover)
ISBN 978-1-62832-196-8 (pbk)
1. Real Madrid Club de Fútbol—
History—Juvenile literature. I. Title.

GV943.6.R35.W47 2014
796.334'64094641—dc23   2014029739

CCSS: RI.5.1, 2, 3, 8; RH.6-8.4, 5, 7

First Edition HC 9 8 7 6 5 4 3 2 1
First Edition PBK 9 8 7 6 5 4 3 2 1

Cover and page 3: Striker Cristiano Ronaldo
Page 1: 2009 La Liga match

CONTENTS

Goalkeeper Iker Casillas

INTRODUCTION

Soccer (or football, as it is known almost everywhere else in the world) is truly a universal game. Nowhere is the play more competitive than in Europe. Almost every European country has its own league, and generally that league has several divisions. A typical season lasts eight or nine months, from late summer to mid-spring. Every team in each level plays all other teams in its level twice, once at home and once on the other team's pitch. At the end of the season, the bottommost teams in one division are relegated (moved down) to the next lower division, with the same number of topmost teams from that lower division promoted to replace them. Such a system ensures that a high level of competition is maintained and that late-season games between teams with losing records remain important as they seek to avoid relegation.

Individual countries also feature their own tournaments, such as England's FA Cup and Spain's Copa del Rey. In theory, these tournaments allow almost any team the opportunity to win the championship, but in reality the best clubs dominate the competition. An assortment of European-wide tournaments complement individual nations' league and cup play. The most prestigious is the Union of European Football Associations (UEFA) Champions League. Known as the European Cup until

WINNERS
UEFA SUPER CUP 2014

Spain's Real Madrid has carved a place for itself among history's most successful football clubs.

1993, the Champions League is a tournament consisting of 32 teams drawn primarily from the highest finishers in the strongest national leagues. Other teams can play their way into the tournament in preliminary rounds. It originated in 1954, when the otherwise obscure Wolverhampton Wanderers of England defeated Honved, the top-rated Hungarian side, prompting Wanderers manager Stan Cullis to declare his team "Champions of the World." Noted French soccer journalist Gabriel Hanot disagreed and helped organize a continent-wide competition that began in 1956.

The Champions League starts with eight four-team pools, which play two games with one another. The top two teams from each pool begin a series of knockout rounds, also contested on a two-game basis. The last two teams play a single championship game at a neutral site. The tournament runs concurrently with league play, beginning in September and concluding in May. Teams that win their league, their national cup, and the Champions League during the same season are said to have won the Continental Treble—almost certainly the most difficult feat in all of professional sports. The winner of the Champions League is eligible for the FIFA Club World Cup, an annual seven-team tournament that originated in 2000. It also includes teams from the Americas and Caribbean, Africa, Asia, Oceania, and the host nation.

The other major European club championship is the UEFA Europa League, founded in 1971 and known as the UEFA Cup until the 2009–10 season. The winners of these two tournaments play for the UEFA Super Cup, usually held in August.

ALL-TIME CHAMPIONS LEAGUE RECORDS OF THE TOP 10 CLUBS (AS OF 2014):

	Winner	Runner-up
Real Madrid (Spain)	10	3
AC Milan (Italy)	7	4
Bayern Munich (Germany)	5	5
Liverpool (England)	5	2
Barcelona (Spain)	4	3
Ajax (Netherlands)	4	2
Manchester United (England)	3	2
Inter Milan (Italy)	3	2
Benfica (Portugal)	2	5
Juventus (Italy)	2	5

Santiago Bernabéu Stadium

CONTINENTAL TREBLE WINNERS

Celtic (Scotland)	1966–67
Ajax (Netherlands)	1971–72
PSV (Netherlands)	1987–88
Manchester United (England)	1998–99
Barcelona (Spain)	2008–09
Inter Milan (Italy)	2009–10
Bayern Munich (Germany)	2012–13

LET'S GET REAL!

The 3,418-room Royal Palace of Madrid, built on the site of Mayrit, served as a residence for Spanish monarchs.

While people have lived on the site of Madrid, Spain, for thousands of years, Muslims built the first major settlement in A.D. 854. They named it Mayrit, from an Arab word meaning "water channel" and referring to the nearby Manzanares River. Christians captured the city in 1085, and it became the Spanish capital in 1561, primarily because of its location at the geographical center of the country. Throughout the centuries, Madrid emerged as one of Europe's showpiece cities. Today, it is especially noted for its many architectural gems and rich culture.

The city also boasts one of the world's best soccer teams, Real Madrid. The team was founded in 1902 as Madrid Football Club (FC). Modern soccer had originated in England several decades earlier, and its influence soon spread to continental Europe. The fledgling Madrid club's first set of rules came from the English city of Manchester. The team's nickname—"Los Blancos"—was derived from its all-white uniforms, copied from a London team. One of the key players, Arthur Johnson, was a London businessman who, according to a contemporary report, "knew more about the game than anybody else. Johnson [was] the captain of the team—he distinguished himself with his tackling, agility, and elegance of body." Johnson's versatility helped him excel all over the pitch, playing center-half, center-forward, and goalkeeper. At age 23, Johnson was also the team's "old man." Homegrown players such as forward

Madrid teams of the early 1900s established the club's reputation by capturing national titles.

Pedro Parages—who later became the team's president—
complemented Johnson's leadership.

When 16-year-old Alfonso XIII was crowned king
of Spain a few weeks after the club was formed, a soccer
tournament called the Coronation Cup became part of
the festivities. In the opening game, FC Barcelona defeated
Madrid 3–1. This was the first recorded meeting of the two
teams that would not only eventually dominate Spanish
soccer but also serve as symbols of two very different
cultures within the nation. Barcelona is the capital of
Catalonia, a self-governing region in northeastern Spain.
El Clásico (the classic)—the name given to games between
the two teams—is likely the world's most intense sports
rivalry. Many historians trace the rivalry's
origins back to 1714, when forces loyal
to Spanish king Philip V
conquered Barcelona after a
lengthy siege. Thousands
of soldiers and civilians
on both sides died in
the conflict, resulting
in long-lasting hostility
between the two cities.
Events in the 20th
century only added fuel to
the fire.

*Alfonso XIII's long reign lasted through such
conflicts as the Spanish-American War.*

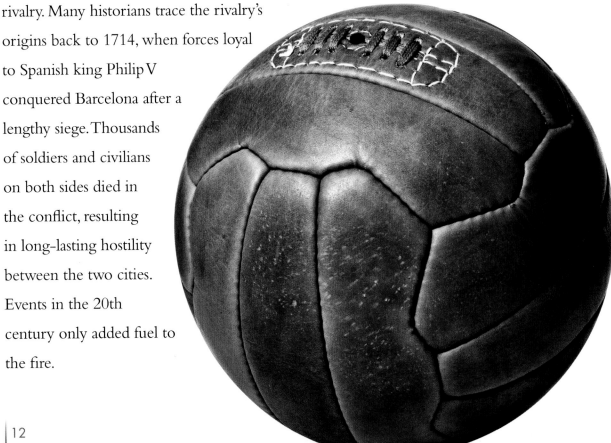

Unlike its 1902 predecessor (top), the current Madrid club crest includes a crown (bottom).

In 1903, the enthusiasm generated by the Coronation Cup resulted in a more permanent tournament, the Copa del Rey (King's Cup). Madrid won the cup for the first time in 1905, and then defended the title the three following years. Originally, the cup was a three- or four-day tournament with a handful of teams. The 1908 cup consisted of a single game, with Madrid defeating Real Vigo Sporting 2–1. By the time Madrid won another title in 1917, the cup had become a Spanish championship lasting for nearly two months.

Five years earlier, one of the most important figures in club history—Santiago Bernabéu—had joined the team. He was just 17 at the time and remained a striker and team captain until 1927. Madrid was also a force in the Campeonato Centro, one of four regions that served to qualify teams for the Copa del Rey. Between 1904 and 1928, Madrid finished in the top 3 of the Campeonato each year, winning the title 15 times.

In 1920, King Alfonso, seeking to improve his standing among his subjects, granted his patronage to several teams, including Madrid. Now Madrid could include the word *real* (*ray-ALL*), meaning "royal," in its name and use the image of a crown in its coat of arms and uniforms. However, this privilege did not sit well with those teams—most notably Barcelona—excluded from the monarch's favor.

THE ARROW AND THE CANNON

Thanks to Madrid's ongoing success, it outgrew its previous facilities and opened the 20,000-seat Chamartín Stadium in 1924. Prince Don Gonzalo kicked the ball of honor and shouted, *"Hala, Madrid!"* (Let's go, Madrid!) The team took the encouragement to heart, defeating Newcastle United, one of England's best teams, by a 3–2 score in the first game. "Hala, Madrid!" would remain the official rallying cry of the team for years to come.

Soccer was becoming increasingly popular in the rest of Spain as well. In 1929, La Liga was founded to provide a nationwide league, though teams still considered their established regional

competitions to be just as important. The new league set up a double round-robin on a home and away basis. Real Madrid was one of the original 10 teams. Although Barcelona won the first championship, Real took home its first two trophies in 1931–32 and 1932–33.

Momentous national events soon took their toll on Spanish soccer. In 1931, elections established the Second Spanish Republic. Five years later, a military takeover of the government plunged the country into a bloody and brutal civil war. It pitted the Republicans (who favored continuing the republic) against the Nationalists, led by Generalissimo Francisco Franco. More than a million

Los Nacionales

MINISTERIO DE PROPAGANDA

Spanish Republicans criticized Nationalist leaders such as Franco (opposite) and other world powers (above).

people on both sides died in the bitter fighting before Franco's forces emerged victorious in 1939. Franco swept into Barcelona—the last Republican stronghold—and executed thousands. Even though Madrid had been solidly Republican during the conflict, Franco established his government there. Franco was especially harsh in his dealings with Catalonia. Its language (Catalan) couldn't be spoken in public, the Catalan flag was banned, and parents were even forbidden from giving Catalan names to newborn boys. The restrictions served to increase the hostility between the respective cities' soccer teams. Tensions peaked in 1943 when Real took home-field advantage to an extreme and annihilated Barcelona 11–1, which was by far the largest margin of victory in El Clásico.

Soon afterward, Santiago Bernabéu became the president of Real Madrid. He inherited a team in shambles. The bleachers in Chamartín Stadium had been ripped out and used for firewood during the civil war, and the rest of the facility was heavily damaged. A number of players and officials had been killed, some of the team's trophies had been stolen, and Real wasn't even the best team in Madrid anymore. That honor went to Atlético de Madrid, which benefited from financial backing from the government and a strong team of former Spanish Air Force members. It took years for Bernabéu to restore Real's fortunes. At his insistence, the club constructed a new facility. Called New Chamartín Stadium (and renamed Santiago Bernabéu Stadium in 1955), it opened in December 1947 as Europe's largest soccer stadium. Able to seat more than 75,000, detractors sneered that it was "too much of a stadium for so little a club."

Nationalist troops overcame Republican fighters north of Madrid before moving south.

The signing of legendary Alfredo Di Stéfano (fourth from left) marked a new era for Real.

Hoping to boost Real's status, Bernabéu signed Argentine forward Alfredo Di Stéfano, nicknamed "Saeta Rubia" (Blond Arrow), in 1953. However, it soon appeared that both Real and Barcelona had a contract with him. After a series of bitter negotiations, Barcelona agreed to give up its claim in exchange for a substantial cash payment. When Di Stéfano emerged as perhaps the greatest player of his generation, the rivalry between the two teams grew even more intense. It remains a sore point among Barcelona fans even today. Soon afterward, Real signed another key player:

Strong-legged Ferenc Puskás proved to be a scoring dynamo, powering shots into the net.

Hungarian striker Ferenc Puskás, who quickly acquired the nickname "Cañoncito Pum" (Little Cannon) for the strength of his shots.

The arrival of these promising players coincided with Real's domination of La Liga. Franco had banned regional competition in 1940, and Real's fortunes in La Liga since then had ranged from a handful of 2nd and 3rd places to as low as 11th. But between 1953 and 1969, Los Blancos were league titlists 12 times and 2nd or 3rd the other 4 seasons.

SIX CUPS: YEAH, YEAH, YEAH!

After Real's victory in 1956's inaugural European Cup, opponents all over the world took notice of the Spanish club.

Di Stéfano and Puskás assumed key roles on an even larger stage as Real Madrid played in the first-ever European Cup final in 1956. Facing France's Stade de Reims, Real fell behind 2–0 in the first 10 minutes. Di Stéfano countered a few minutes later, and striker Héctor Rial evened the game at the 30-minute mark. Reims regained the lead in the second half, but defender Marcos Alonso brought Real back to an even footing soon afterward. Rial fired home the game-winner with 11 minutes remaining to give Real the trophy with a 4–3 win. The victory launched a five-year Cup winning streak, unmatched as of 2014. Playing at Bernabéu Stadium the following year against Fiorentina of Italy, Real rode a pair of second-half goals by Di Stéfano and forward Francisco Gento to a 2–0 win.

The scene shifted to Brussels, Belgium, for the 1958 European Cup final. After a goalless first half, Italy's AC Milan scored in the 59th minute. Di Stéfano tied the game 15 minutes later, Milan retaliated within 3 minutes, and Rial brought Madrid even once again 2 minutes afterward. Gento scored the game-winner in extra time.

Di Stéfano helped Los Blancos secure an impressive haul of five consecutive European Cup trophies from 1956 to 1960.

"I received the ball in the [penalty] area, and I hit it very hard," Gento recalled, "and it went through lots of legs and into the net. It was a big surprise to see it in the net." The 1959 game, played in Stuttgart, Germany, was a rematch of the first finals against Stade de Reims. Striker Enrique Mateos and Di Stéfano each scored to help Real to its fourth title. That set the stage in 1960 for what many observers call the best ever European soccer game, as Real demolished Eintracht Frankfurt of Germany 7–3.

For Franco, Real's value was incalculable. "Goals broadcast by radio were more effective trumpets of triumph than the anthem [of Franco's political party] 'Cara al Sol,'" notes author Eduardo Galeano. "In 1959, one of the regime's political bosses, José Solís, voiced his gratitude to the players: 'Thanks to you, people who used to hate us now understand us.' Like El Cid [a medieval military leader and Spanish national hero], Real Madrid embodied all the virtues of Immortal Spain."

With some of its stars beginning to age, the club signed younger players such as 22-year-old striker Amancio Amaro, quickly nicknamed "El Brujo" (The Wizard).

Midfielder Raymond Kopa, Rial, Di Stéfano, Puskás, and Gento (left to right) played together in 1959.

Di Stéfano notched Madrid's first goal in the 1960 European Cup final before adding two more against Eintracht.

Real returned to the European Cup final in 1962, playing Portugal's Benfica. Los Blancos appeared on their way to another win, with Puskás notching a hat trick in the first half to give Real a 3–2 lead. But Benfica fought back, and its rising star Eusébio—who would become one of the world's greatest players—scored the game's last two goals as his team won 5–3.

After shocking the soccer world with an exit in the early rounds of the 1963 European Cup, Real powered its way back to the finals against Inter Milan of Italy the following year. Inter defender Giacinto Facchetti realized what his team was up against. "To play Real Madrid against such great players as Di Stéfano, Puskás, and Gento was hard for us," he said later. "We were youngsters, and it was difficult to play against a great team." Not too difficult, however, to take a 2–0 lead early in the second half.

Eager for redemption, Real players were prepared to win the 1966 European Cup final.

After Real midfielder Rafael Batista Hernández brought his team within one goal, Inter took advantage of a defensive error in front of the Real net to clinch the game 3–1.

Real wouldn't be denied in its bid for a sixth European Cup in 1966 against Partizan of Belgrade, Yugoslavia. Partizan scored early in the second half, but goals by Amaro and midfielder Fernando Serena gave Los Blancos a 2–1 win. Gento became the first player to have six winners' medals. "I have always looked after myself and carried on playing until I was 38 years old," he said. "I played in European Cup games for 15 years, and I've won a record of 6 finals out of the 8 I played in. As a footballer, you can't really ask for more." Los Blancos picked up another nickname that year when four members appeared in a photo wearing Beatles wigs. With the Beatles at the height of their popularity, Real took on the nickname "Ye-Yé," after the refrain ("Yeah, yeah, yeah") from the hit single "She Loves You".

FROM VULTURES TO *GALÁCTICOS*

No one realized it at the time, but Real would be "no, no, no" for more than 30 years in European Cup competition. However, Los Blancos remained a force in La Liga, taking the title six times from 1971–72 to 1979–80. A key player during this era was forward Juanito. "Playing for Real Madrid is like touching the sky," he said. "Real Madrid has always been my first choice as a team, and Madrid has always been my favorite as a city." German-born midfielder/sweeper Uli Stielike, nicknamed "The Stopper," anchored the defense.

Uli Stielike, known for his smart and aggressive style on the pitch, spent eight seasons playing for Madrid.

After five seasons without a La Liga title in the early 1980s, Los Blancos ran off a string of five championships in a row from 1986 to 1990. The team was headed by striker Emilio "The Vulture" Butragueño. He and four other players who all came up through Real's youth academy—sweeper Manolo Sanchís, attacking midfielder Rafael Martín Vázquez, midfielder Míchel, and forward Miguel Pardeza—were known collectively as "La Quinta del Buitre" (The Vulture's Cohort). With Mexican import Hugo Sánchez winning an unprecedented four consecutive Pichichi trophies as La Liga's scoring leader during this time, *France Football* magazine labeled Real as the best European team of the decade. While the European Cup drought continued despite three semifinals appearances in a row, Los Blancos won two Copas del Rey, finished second twice, and made the semifinals four times during the decade. Real also won back-to-back UEFA Cup championships, taking the 1984–85 title over Hungary's Videoton and knocking off the German side FC Köln the following year.

Real won two more La Liga titles in the 1990s and finally reappeared in the 1997–98 finals of the European Cup, now known as the Champions League (although the actual trophy was still called the European Cup). Real was a considerable underdog following a humdrum record in La Liga play, while Italian rival Juventus had won the Cup in 1996 and taken second the following year. The game was remarkably even—Real controlled the ball 51 percent of the time and took eight shots to Juventus's nine. In the 66th minute, Real striker Predrag Mijatović reacted to a deflection and sidestepped Juventus keeper Angelo Peruzzi for the game-winning goal. Taking note that the club had now won more than 50 major trophies, the International Federation of Association Football (FIFA), the governing body of international soccer, named Real Madrid the "Best Club in History" later that year. Di Stéfano and Puskás were honored among the sport's 10 best players of all time.

Midfielder Fernando Redondo was the 2000 Champions League's Most Valuable Player.

Real Madrid made history in 2000 by facing Valencia of Spain in the first Champions League final pitting two teams from the same country against each other. A poorly cleared free kick led to a header from Real striker Fernando Morientes in the 39th minute. Attacking midfielder Steve McManaman's volley from the edge of the penalty area gave Real a 2–0 lead midway through the second half. With Valencia throwing all its resources forward, striker Raúl took a clearing pass most of the length of the field, dribbled around the keeper, and tapped in the game's final goal.

Fan favorite David Beckham punched in 20 goals during his time with Los Blancos.

A new era began soon afterward when Florentino Pérez, the owner of Spain's largest construction company, became president in 2000. By reorganizing the team's finances, he made Real the world's richest club. He used the money to assemble a team nicknamed Los Galácticos for its "star" power: attacking midfielder Luís Figo (signed in 2000), attacking midfielder Zinedine Zidane (2001), Brazilian striker Ronaldo (2002), and midfielder David Beckham (2003). The policy was successful, as Real won La Liga in 2000–01 and 2002–03 along with its third Champions League crown in five years in 2001–02.

DIM STARS BRIGHTENED AGAIN

Despite all the on-field talent, the team's long drought in Copa del Rey competition—the last title had been in 1992–93—continued. Fans became restless when three years passed without any major trophies. When Real was bounced in the round of 16 in the 2005–06 Champions League without scoring a goal in either game, Pérez resigned. Though Real narrowly won La Liga the following season, Beckham, the last of the original Galácticos, left to join the Los Angeles Galaxy.

Real felt especially humiliated in 2008–09: an early exit in the Copa del Rey by third-level Real Unión, a 5–0 thumping by Liverpool in the Champions League first knockout round, and a pair of El Clásico losses. Most galling was Barcelona winning the Continental Treble—the first Spanish team to do so—and adding three additional trophies by the end of 2009 in what was termed "The Magic Year." Pérez signed on as team president and promised to restore Real to glory by doing what he did best: spending money. With Pérez's return, the second Galácticos era began.

In short order, Real signed defender Raúl Albiol, striker Karim Benzema, and midfielder Xabi Alonso. That was just the warm-up. Pérez soon broke his own records for transfer fees by signing players from two of the top European

Kaká (right) later called former teammate Cristiano Ronaldo (left) the best footballer he had ever played with.

clubs. First came attacking midfielder Kaká from AC Milan, and then a few weeks later, forward Cristiano Ronaldo from Manchester United.

All the pieces didn't fall into place immediately. Though Real set a team record of 96 points in the 2009–10 La Liga season, Barcelona won the title with just a single defeat and 99 points. Second-division Alcorcón knocked off Real 4–1 in the Copa del Rey's round of 32. And again, Real lost in the round of 16 in the Champions League.

The situation improved the following season. Real Madrid won the Copa del Rey and reached the semifinals of the Champions League but once again finished second to Barcelona in La Liga. Everything came together in the 2011–12 La Liga campaign.

Real established new records for points (100), wins (32), goals scored (121), and goal differential (89). Los Blancos also had the satisfaction of defeating Barcelona 2–1 on its home field. In Champions League play, however, Real lost to German powerhouse Bayern Munich in the semifinals on penalty kicks.

Unfortunately for Real, Barcelona matched the 100-point record in the following La Liga season and ran away with the title. Once again, Los Blancos reached the Champions League semifinals, only to lose to Germany's Borussia Dortmund. Noting that his nearly bankrupt club could afford only a young, homegrown lineup against Real's expensive roster, Dortmund manager Jürgen Klopp termed the result "like Robin Hood taking from the rich." Pitted against Atlético de Madrid in the Copa del Rey final, Real fell 2–1 in extra time.

The team did even better in 2013–14. Real inked 24-year-old winger Gareth Bale with yet another record transfer fee to begin the season. The expectation was that Bale would team with Benzema and Ronaldo to give Los Blancos the most formidable scoring punch in European soccer. A 4–0 drubbing of Real Valladolid in November 2013 helped demonstrate the effectiveness of this combination. Bale scored a "perfect" hat trick—left foot, right foot, header—and assisted on a Benzema goal. Promising young talent such as defender Raphaël Varane and attacking midfielder Isco contributed as well.

In mid-April, Los Blancos won the Copa del Rey in yet another El Clásico, defeating their archrivals 2–1 on a late goal by Bale. Later that month, the team demolished Champions League favorite Bayern Munich 5–0 to reach the final. But after topping the standings for much of the season, Real dropped to third in La Liga with two ties and a loss in May. Los Blancos hoped to make amends by defeating Atlético de Madrid in the first-ever Champions League final matching teams from the same city. Relying on its stout defense, Atlético seemed on the verge of making a 1–0 halftime

Gareth Bale used both his speed and his skillful footwork to outmatch opponents.

Defensive powerhouse Sergio Ramos brought acrobatics to Real when he arrived in 2005.

lead stand up. But with two minutes left in stoppage time, Real defender Sergio Ramos headed in a corner kick to send the game into extra time. With 10 minutes left, winger/midfielder Ángel Di María split two defenders near the goal and launched a shot. The Atlético keeper deflected it, but Bale soared high into the air to head the ball into the upper-right corner of the net. Real added two more goals in the final two minutes to seal a 4–1 victory—and La Décima ("the tenth" European Cup).

"Overcoming every challenge is in our DNA," said jubilant club president Pérez afterward. "The best thing about this club is the culture of the fans, which is passed down from parents to their children, who will already be thinking about the 11th European Cup." Real Madrid fans will also be thinking about the Continental Treble, La Liga, Copa del Rey—and perhaps above all, El Clásico. Achieving success at the expense of FC Barcelona would certainly make any of those triumphs all the sweeter.

MEMORABLE MATCHES

1902

Team was founded.

1916

Madrid v. FC Barcelona

El Clásico, March–April, 1916, Barcelona and Madrid, Spain

According to many soccer authorities, the animosity that characterizes El Clásico dates back to the semifinals of the 1916 Copa del Rey. Even though Barcelona won the first game 2–1, its players complained about the referee. After Madrid took the next game 4–1, Barcelona had even more reasons for unhappiness. The Royal Spanish Football Association announced that the tiebreaker to decide the finalist would be played in Atlético de Madrid's O'Donnell stadium. Barcelona fans and officials protested because they felt it gave Real an unfair advantage. Two Real players—including future club president Santiago Bernabéu—scored hat tricks in a 6–6 tie. Bernabéu's final goal came with three minutes left when Barcelona was penalized for a hand ball—a call its players bitterly protested. The following day, the teams battled to a 2–2 tie in regulation time. Madrid scored twice in extra time, but Barcelona demanded that the second score—with seven minutes remaining—be disallowed because of offside. When the referee refused, Barcelona players stormed off the field. Madrid was declared the winner, though Los Blancos lost the final to Athletic Bilbao 4–0.

Real Madrid v. Barcelona
Copa del Rey, June 21, 1936, Valencia, Spain

The year 1936 marked the first meeting of Madrid and Barcelona in a Copa del Rey final (known as the Copa del Presidente de la República from 1931 to 1939). Real forward Eugenio Hilario opened the scoring 6 minutes into the game, and forward Simón Lecue added a goal at the 12-minute mark. Barcelona's José Escolà halved the margin about 15 minutes later. With the score still 2–1 in the game's waning moments, Escolà sent a low, hard drive toward the far post. All 22,000 spectators jumped to their feet in anticipation of a tie game. Madrid's keeper Ricardo Zamora dove to his left, stirring up a cloud of dust that momentarily obscured the scene. When it cleared, Zamora stood calmly in front of the goal, holding the ball and preserving the win. The photograph of the save is probably the most famous image in Spanish soccer history. Jubilant fans carried Zamora off the field. It was his last game with Los Blancos, as he fled to France during the civil war. It was also one of the last soccer games before the outbreak of brutal conflict.

Real Madrid v. Barcelona
Copa del Generalissimo Semifinals, June 13, 1943, Madrid, Spain

Barcelona won the first leg of the 1943 Copa del Rey (renamed for dictator Franco as the Copa del Generalissimo) 3–0 at home, subjecting Real to a constant barrage of booing and catcalls. When the action shifted to Madrid, Real fans threatened retaliation. Barcelona players feared for their lives if they left their hotel. Before the game, Franco's director of state security delivered a barely veiled threat of exile or imprisonment. As play began, the home crowd was even more hostile than Barcelona's. The result was an 11–1 Real landside, which remains the largest margin of victory between the two teams. "Barça [Barcelona] simply ended up by not playing at all," wrote young journalist Juan Antonio Samaranch. "Individual players were fearful of making the most innocent of tackles because of the crowd reaction.... It was frankly sad having to watch the spectacle of a Barcelona team forcefully reduced to impotence by the coercion of the crowd." Samaranch's article drew outrage from Real Madrid supporters, and he was fired. But it didn't hurt his long-term career. In 1980, Samaranch became head of the International Olympic Committee.

1960

Real Madrid v. Eintracht Frankfurt
European Cup Final, May 18, 1960, Glasgow, Scotland

Played before a record crowd of more than 127,000, the 1960 European Cup final nearly didn't take place. Angered by allegations from Real's Ferenc Puskás that the 1954 West German national team had taken illegal drugs, the German Football Association banned its member teams from playing against him. The organization relented when Puskás apologized. In hindsight, Eintracht probably wished he hadn't. Only three players have hat tricks in Cup finals, and two came in this game. Frankfurt opened the scoring, but Real forward Alfredo Di Stéfano retaliated with two goals in a three-minute span. Puskás added a third just before halftime, and then overwhelmed Frankfurt with 3 second-half goals within 16 minutes. Frankfurt answered, but Di Stéfano completed his hat trick a few moments later. Frankfurt scored the game's final goal—the fourth time the nets had been dented within four minutes—but there was no doubt as to which team was superior. "Eintracht found themselves playing Spanish supermen, and I don't think I ever saw anything like the performance Real put on that night," said Rangers (Scotland) player Davie Wilson. "The Spaniards had 11 players who possessed everything."

2002

Real Madrid v. Bayer Leverkusen

Champions League Final, May 15, 2002, Glasgow, Scotland

In its centennial year, Real Madrid had failed to win either La Liga or the Copa del Rey. The Champions League final was the club's last opportunity to honor the occasion with a major trophy. History seemed to be on the side of Los Blancos, with the game held at Hampden Park—the site of their 7–3 demolition of Eintracht Frankfurt 42 years earlier. This game, however, was much more competitive. Striker Raúl put Real ahead eight minutes into the match, but Germany's Leverkusen provided the equalizer five minutes later. Just before halftime, Real attacking midfielder Zinedine Zidane took a cross from left-back Roberto Carlos at the top of the penalty area, pivoted on his right foot, and volleyed the ball into the net with his left foot. "You only score a goal like that once in your life," Zidane said. "I'm so proud and happy it happened to me. You can try something like that a hundred times, and it'll only come off once." Substitute keeper Iker Casillas helped preserve the victory with three saves in second-half stoppage time as Real won its ninth title, 2–1.

2011

Real Madrid v. Barcelona

Copa del Rey, April 20, 2011, Valencia, Spain

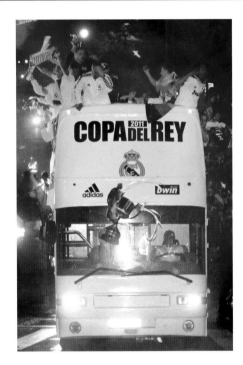

The 2011 Copa del Rey marked the sixth Copa final between Spain's two football giants. It was also the midpoint of an unprecedented 11-day span of 3 El Clásicos. Real dominated the first half but couldn't score. In the second half, Barcelona superstar Lionel Messi created numerous scoring chances, requiring Real keeper Iker Casillas to make several spectacular saves. Regulation time ended in a scoreless tie. In extra time, Real winger/midfielder Ángel Di María sent a left-footed cross more than half the width of the field to forward Cristiano Ronaldo, who headed the ball into the goal from about 12 yards out. It marked Real's first win over its archrival since 2008. During the victory parade that night, defender Sergio Ramos hoisted the cup in front of the cheering crowd. But he lost control of the 30-pound and 3-foot-high trophy, and it tumbled in front of the bus carrying the team, reducing it to scrap metal. Ramos joked, "It didn't fall; it jumped when it got to Cibeles [a Madrid city square] and saw so many Madristas [Real Madrid fans]."

FAMOUS FOOTBALLERS

RICARDO ZAMORA

(1901–78)
Keeper, 1930–36

Though Ricardo Zamora arrived in Madrid at the end of his career—which had included three seasons with Barcelona—his skills were undimmed, and he remained known as "The Divine One." According to soccer writer Eduardo Galeano, "He sowed panic among strikers. If they looked his way, they were lost: with Zamora in the goal, the net would shrink, and the posts would lose themselves in the distance…. For 20 years, he was the best goalkeeper in the world." He also had one of the most distinctive uniforms of any keeper: turtleneck sweater and cloth cap. "Zamora was more famous in his day than [movie star] Greta Garbo, and better looking," remarked teammate Jacinto Quincoces. "He was certainly a better goalkeeper." Despite his status, Zamora nearly became a casualty of the Spanish Civil War. Suspected of being pro-Franco, he was imprisoned by Republican forces. At one point, a radio broadcast reported that he had been executed. To ease the tension, he played soccer games with other inmates and guards before international efforts finally succeeded in securing his freedom. Today, the Ricardo Zamora Trophy honors Spain's best keeper each season.

SANTIAGO BERNABÉU

(1895–1978)
Striker, 1913–27
Manager, 1936–41
President, 1943–78

Santiago Bernabéu began watching Real Madrid matches as a boy and joined the junior team at the age of 14. He made his debut with the senior team three years later. At first, the coaches wanted him to be the team's keeper, but his older brother Marcelo—a cofounder of the club—convinced them Santiago was better suited as striker. During his 14-year career—much of it as captain—Bernabéu scored 69 goals in 78 games. He served as manager for several years and became team president in 1943. Recognizing the need for a new stadium, Bernabéu was able to raise the necessary funds despite severe economic conditions following the civil war. Perhaps his greatest legacy was forming the first truly international club team by importing a number of foreign-born players. Among his most important signings was forward Alfredo Di Stéfano in 1953 as he helped turn Real into a global powerhouse. Bernabéu also played a key role in establishing the European Cup. When he died during the 1978 World Cup, FIFA officials honored his contributions to soccer with three official days of mourning amidst the tournament.

ALFREDO DI STÉFANO

(1926–2014)
Forward, 1953–64

From the moment he began playing in his native Argentina, Alfredo Di Stéfano seemed destined for greatness. He attracted the attention of both Barcelona and Real Madrid during an exhibition in 1952. In a controversial transfer that compounded the hostility between the two clubs, Di Stéfano joined Los Blancos and almost immediately helped catapult the team to the top ranks of European soccer. He scored 418 goals in 510 appearances with Real and nearly 900 during his career. In 1999, Di Stéfano was voted the fourth-best soccer player of the century, trailing only Pelé, Johan Cruyff, and Diego Maradona. Pelé termed Di Stéfano "the most complete footballer in the history of the game." An indication of Di Stéfano's towering reputation among his contemporaries came from the great Portuguese player Eusébio. After scoring the winning goal against Real in the 1962 European Cup, 19-year-old Eusébio had just one thing in mind: getting his personal hero's jersey. Decades later, in a home packed with testimonials to his own accomplishments, Eusébio remarked, "Di Stéfano's shirt is still the most prized souvenir I have from football."

FERENC PUSKÁS

(1927–2006)
Forward, 1958–66

One of the most prolific goal-scorers of all time, Ferenc Puskás was an unlikely star. As Jack Bell of the *New York Times* noted, "Puskás did not have the look of a world-class athlete—he was short, stocky, barrel-chested and appeared to be overweight. He rarely headed the ball and used only one foot—a lethal left." These apparent handicaps didn't prevent Puskás from becoming a star on the highly regarded Hungarian team of the early 1950s. When Soviet troops crushed the Hungarian uprising in 1956, Puskás defected to the West. He joined Real 2 years later at the relatively advanced age of 31, teaming with forward Alfredo Di Stéfano for what may have been the greatest one-two punch in soccer history. In his first year with Los Blancos, Puskás showed what was to come when he scored four hat tricks. In both La Liga and European Cup play, Puskás averaged nearly a goal every game. He won the Pichichi—given to La Liga's top scorer—in 1960, 1961, 1963, and 1964. Today, the FIFA Puskás Award honors the man or woman judged to have scored the best goal each season.

LUÍS FIGO

(1972–)
Midfielder, 2000–05

When Luís Figo moved to Real Madrid following five seasons in Barcelona where he was known as the "Lion King" for his leadership, Barcelona fans felt betrayed. Before his first appearance with Real in Barcelona against his former team in 2000, a newspaper printed a photo of his ear, captioned "Figo, they're going to make your ears burn." The stands were packed with fans holding enlarged copies of a 5,000-peseta note, featuring a photo of Figo with the words "Figo, money-grabber!" Whenever the midfielder approached a corner of the pitch, fans screamed, "Die, Figo!" and bombarded him with cell phones, chunks of brick, coins, bicycle chains, and other potentially dangerous objects. After a calm 2001, the vitriol resumed the following year. Surrounded by riot police, Figo needed nearly 15 minutes to take a corner kick. Every time he approached the ball, trash rained down—including, most notoriously, a pig's head. Anger aside, Figo is regarded as one of the finest midfielders in European soccer history and was named FIFA World Player of the Year in 2001. He helped Real win two La Liga titles and a European Cup.

CRISTIANO RONALDO

(1985–)
Forward, 2009–present

Cristiano Ronaldo or Lionel Messi. One or the other won the prestigious Ballon d'Or award six years in a row: Ronaldo in 2008 and 2013, Messi the four intervening years. Ronaldo's illustrious career almost didn't happen. He was diagnosed with a heart condition at age 15, but surgery fortunately cured the problem. He joined Manchester United three years later, helping the team maintain its English Premier League dominance. After the 2007–08 season, Ronaldo won the Ballon d'Or (then known as the FIFA World Player of the Year award) as well as the European Golden Shoe award as the league's leading scorer. When he duplicated the feat in his first season with Real, he became the first player to win the Golden Shoe in two different leagues. (He tied for the Shoe again in 2014.) He went on to average more than a goal a game with Los Blancos. "Ronaldo is easily the best player in the world," said Manchester United coach Alex Ferguson when Ronaldo transferred to Real. "His stats are incredible. Strikes at goal, attempts on goal, raids into the penalty box, headers. It is all there."

REAL MADRID TITLES
THROUGH 2014

**EUROPEAN CUP/
CHAMPIONS
LEAGUE**

Winner
1956
1957
1958
1959
1960
1966
1998
2000
2002
2014
Total: 10

Runner-up
1962
1964
1981
Total: 3

**SUPERCOPA
DE ESPAÑA**

1988
1989
1990
1993
1997
2001
2003
2008
2012
Total: 9